My Map

Written by Jerry Moore
Illustrated by Chris Brown

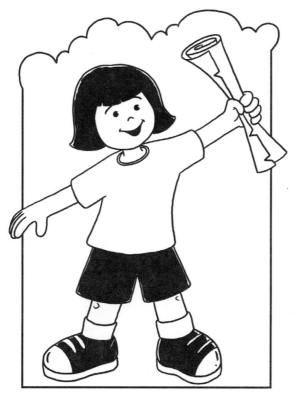

Phonics Skill

Consonant Pp /p/

| Pam | map | tap | pat |

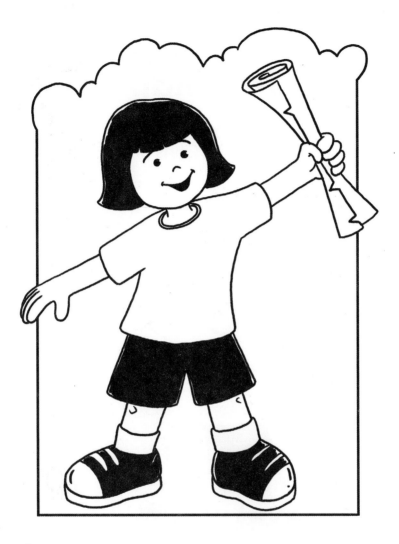

I am Pam.

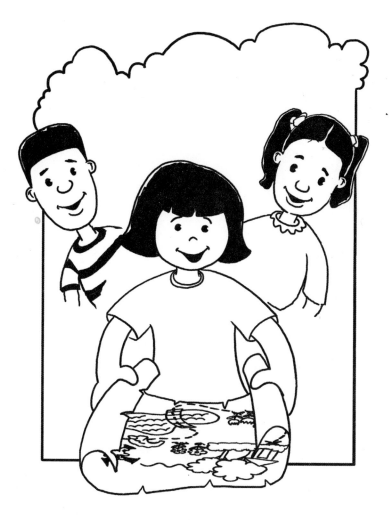

I have a map.

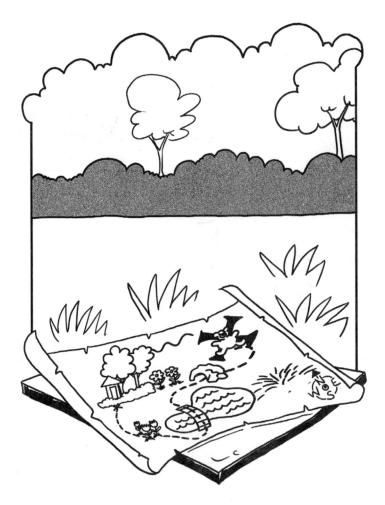

The map sat at the mat.

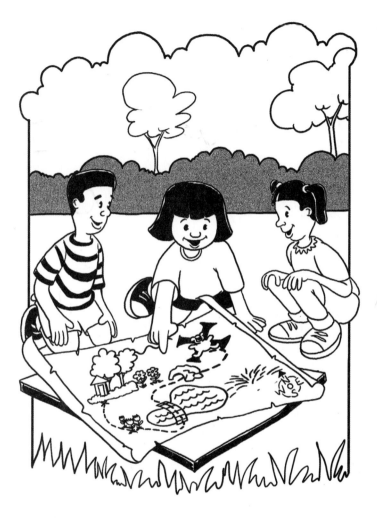

I tap my map.

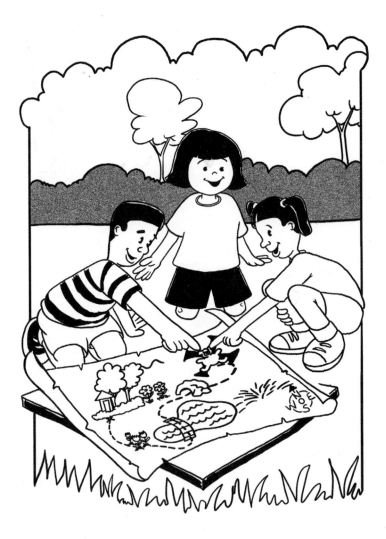

We tap the map.

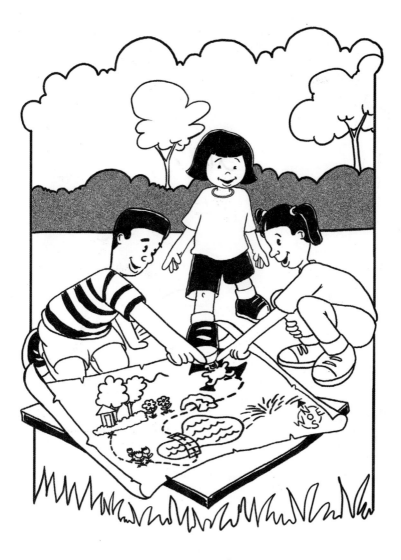

We pat at the map.

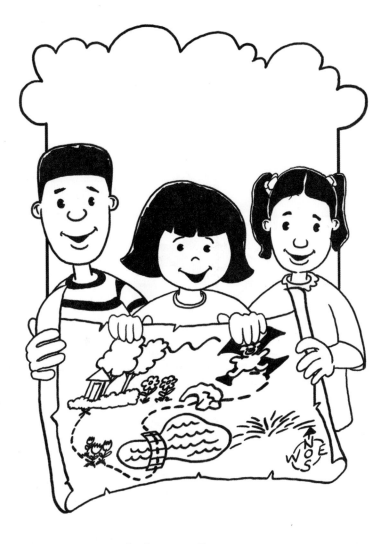

We like the map.